FROM BAD CAT
TO GOOD CAT
IN 21 DAYS

FROM BAD CAT TO GOOD CAT IN 21 DAYS

An Owner's Guide to CAT LITTERBOX REHABILITATION

98% Proven Success Rate

Diane Arrington

Copyright © 1986, 2014 by Diane Arrington

CATPAN 2000

A PetPerfect® Book

Photo by Diane Arrington
Graphic design by Tatiana Villa

ISBN 978-1629670652

The information in this book is distributed on an "as is" basis, without warranty. Although every precaution has been taken in the preparation of this work, neither the author nor the publisher shall have any liability to any person or entity with respect to any loss or damage caused or alleged to be caused directly or indirectly by the information contained in this book.

Also by Diane Arrington:

Seventh Sense

Unbroken Spirits

Grubby Goes to Furville

For Kewee, the most perfect creature God ever created.

CONTENTS

OVERVIEW
1

CHAPTER ONE
PHASE I – The Retraining Procedure
5

CHAPTER TWO
The Exit Program – A Crucial Step
29

CHAPTER THREE
PHASE II – The Exit Program Procedure
32

SUPPLY LIST
40

QUICK-REFERENCE GUIDE
41

ABOUT THE AUTHOR
43

OVERVIEW

There is no data available that determines precisely the number of cats killed annually across the United States and Europe as a result of cat litterbox problems, but the numbers range in the millions. Feline inappropriate elimination is the leading cause of death in cats. Millions have been destroyed needlessly. This most common and most offensive behavior problem among felines can be treated. A litterbox problem is not a death sentence. Don't consider euthanasia until you have followed this rehabilitation program exactly.

CATPAN 2000© is a culmination of more than two hundred cases involving litterbox retraining. It can be used to address all three of inappropriate elimination: urination, defecation and spraying (scent marking). When followed with precision, and assuming the cat has no chronic medical condition, this program has proven successful in 99% of defecation, 98% of urination, and 96% of scent-marking.

Rather than try one possible causative factor at a time, we have incorporated into one behavior program all factors that have historically been known to create a barrier to litterbox re-entry, shortening recovery time by eight weeks. This program should take 3-5 weeks, and has been successful in retraining even older cats who have maintained the problem since adoption.

The CATPAN 2000© program uses confinement as the critical avenue to recovery. This portion of the program is an emotional issue for cat owners and lovers. We are aware of client reluctance to restrict the freedom of their cats.

Let us reassure you from the beginning that negative behavioral side effects caused by the confinement phase of this program are rare. In fact, quite the opposite is often true. We generally see seven so-called 'side effects' of the program. Cats become generally more resilient, more affectionate, more tolerant to handling, begin to pay more attention to personal hygiene, become more efficient about covering in the litterbox, grow more playful, and develop a general demeanor that is friendlier and happier. Many of our clients have remarked that their older cats have turned into 'kittens' again as a result of this program.

As you glance through this program you may feel you have already tried everything suggested so why bother. Many people have tried most of it – one thing at a time. In our early history of handling cat litterbox cases we discovered that trying one suggestion at a time piece-meal didn't work, but when we did everything at once it did work. You can set yourself up for failure and a lifetime of cat waste outside of the box – or not. You have nothing to lose by trying. Please read through the entire program before beginning.

FROM BAD CAT TO GOOD CAT IN 21 DAYS

Follow the designated program precisely for optimum success.

In multi-cat households, the offending cat must be determined with certainty before beginning this program. If more than one cat offends, each cat must receive its own individualized program so that owners can determine how each cat is progressing.

NOTE: Before embarking on this program, it is imperative that a veterinarian examine your cat for possible medical causes for the inappropriate behavior. *"I don't think she's sick"* is a layman's opinion and rules out nothing. Possible medical causes must be ruled out with certainty by a veterinary professional.

It is necessary that veterinary determination of the cat's health status be made within two weeks prior to beginning this program. A checkup two or three months prior is inadequate, as cats can develop medical problems in a matter of weeks or even days.

For cats who are only urinating outside the box, fecal must be checked as well. For cats who are only defecating outside the box, urinary must be checked as well. For cats who are spraying, both must be checked. All breeds must have anal glands checked for impaction, inflammation or infection. With Maine Coon cats, check for hip dysplasia.

CATPAN 2000© assumes the patient to be medically sound. Start with a urinalysis, fecal

analysis and anal gland check. If in the end the program does not work for your cat, follow up with a more thorough examination of possible medical causes.

CHAPTER ONE

PHASE I
The Retraining Procedure

The overlying cause of a cat litterbox problem is anxiety stemming from either medical or environmental causes.

PHASE I OBJECTIVES

- Rule out all medical causes
- Eliminate anxiety in the environment
- Make the box more inviting
- Eliminate scent triggers from environment
- Break the connection with the target areas
- Change strata orientation by preventing accidents for two weeks
- Extinguish the behavior and create a new habit
- Stimulate the secretion of endorphins
- Repair broken bonds

PHASE I PROCEDURE

1. Rule out medical causes.

94% of inappropriate elimination cases we see are brought on by a medical condition. The other 6% are triggered by environmental causes.

It will be necessary to rule out urinary, intestinal, digestive and anal gland disorders as possible medical causes. While you are at the veterinarian's office it is simple to also rule out ear infections, tooth decay and any other medical condition that may be causing physical discomfort leading to anxiety. Blood work will not be necessary at this point unless required to rule out these conditions.

2. Eliminate anxiety. Discontinue all scolding or punishment of any kind. This includes shouting, hitting, shaking, loud clapping, rattling penny cans, throwing things at the cat, shock mats, water sprayers and hissing air cans.

Inappropriate elimination in cats is caused by anxiety, be it medical or environmental. Litterbox failure cannot be disciplined out of cats. Cats are dignified animals. Abusive handling is undue and useless. Rubbing a pet's nose in her own excrement is inhumane, unsanitary, and doesn't even work with dogs. Cats do not go out of their boxes deliberately just to make you angry. Errant behavior is a signal. Your cat is suffering. Such treatment will only make the problem worse by increasing anxiety, thereby defeating your purpose.

Eliminating anxiety will be particularly important for cats who are spraying or scent-marking.

Next, we will make the litterbox more inviting.

3. Separate food and water from the box.

First, be sure to separate food and water from the box. Placing the cat food near the litterbox is a surprisingly common mistake. Food and water should be separated from the box by at least six to eight feet if on the same level with the box, but can be closer if it is placed on a counter or other surface above the litterbox.

4. Provide a large enough box.

We have found undersized cat boxes to be one of the leading causes of cat litterbox problems. The bigger the box, the more inviting to a cat. Taking care of her waste is important to a cat, so provide for her what she needs: a nice, roomy area. Even if your cat is still using her box for one or the other of urination or defecation, provide her a large box.

The box should be about 1 1/2 times the length of your cat. Pet stores do not customarily carry boxes large enough. Container stores, department stores and garden stores carry storage boxes the size you will need. For most cats you will need a box that is at least 22 inches long, 17 inches wide and seven inches deep or larger. In multi-cat households, one of these large boxes for every two cats should be sufficient. If your cat sprays, get a box with higher sides.

5. Remove box cover.

A cover over the box will make the box seem smaller in your cat's perception. Cats who prefer a covered box are in the minority. We suggest uncovering the box, at least for the period of this behavior program. You can cover it again later if you wish.

6. Remove plastic liners for the period of the program.

This item is not always essential to the success of CATPAN 2000©, but with cats that are not de-clawed, we have seen it make a difference. Occasionally claws get hung up in the liner, making covering difficult. You can reintroduce the liner at a later date if you choose. (The box size suggested above fits ideally inside a leaf bag.)

7. Use natural, non-clumping, non-deodorized litter 4-5 inches deep.

No adult deaths have been documented, but it has been reported that the sand or clumping-type litter materials have been responsible for a certain number of deaths among small kittens. Cats will ingest anything that might stick to their fur or paws. Clumping litters are fine-grained and easily stick to the paws of a cat. It is reasonable to expect that, when mixed with body fluids, clumping sand litter that has been ingested may also clump inside the gut. This is a danger cat owners should be aware of.

Our research has shown that the majority of cats prefer non-clumping to clumping litter. Even if you have a cat who had a problem with the de-claw operation, use natural, non-clumping clay litter for the period of this program.

Natural ground clay cat litter can be purchased at pet stores, department stores like Target, and even some grocery stores. The ingredients listed on the bag will say, 'natural clay' or 'ground clay.' That's it.

Regardless if you have read that clay litter can harm your cat or the environment, use it for now. It's only for about two or three weeks. When the cat is back in her box, you can gradually replace the clay with your usual litter if you choose. If at that point your cat goes back out of her box, she doesn't like the litter you like.

Use non-deodorized litter because the chlorophyll in deodorized litter can irritate the lining of feline nostrils. Natural clay litter is also more absorbent and does more to combat odors than deodorized litter.

Make the litter four to five inches deep. We have found that the deeper the litter the more absorbent it seems to a cat. It is the natural instinct of both dogs and cats to deposit their waste on an absorbent surface so that the odor will remain longer and discourage competitors from entering the area. A few inches of litter is more inviting to a cat than a few grains at the bottom of a hard plastic box.

If you have a cat you found as a stray, sprinkling a bit of dirt, leaves or grass clippings on top of the clay can sometimes get these cats started by imitating the scent and texture of their previous outdoor experience.

The same is true of cats who have been accustomed to eliminating on a potty pad. Putting a piece of soiled potty pad on top of the clay litter should draw her back into her box.

8. 'Bait' the fresh litter with a few drops of plain ammonia or use any granular, non-clumping cat-attract litter.

Ammonia is a component of urine and will attract the cat to the box in the same way it attracts a cat back to an inappropriate target area in your home. Be certain to use plain pharmacy ammonia, not lemon-scented. Two teaspoons along the top of the litter at program initiation should be sufficient. You will not need to repeat this step. Ammonia can be damaging to the lungs. Cats don't regenerate lung tissue, so do not overdo or repeat the ammonia treatment unless otherwise instructed to do so.

9. Scoop and stir the litter daily, but don't change the litter for two weeks.

You may have read that keeping the litter pristine is the best way to get your cat into the box. This is not necessarily the case. You may be relieved to know that the box does not need to be whistle clean at all times. Changing the cat litter daily is unnecessary in the highest majority of cases. If the litter is pristine at all times, the cat habituates to a perfectly clean litterbox. Then when you get busy and forget to scoop and she hops in the box and finds a lump or two in there, she may be startled and choose not to use the box.

When a cat urinates in clay, urine collects and 'lumps' at the bottom. Stirring this into the rest of the litter each day will aid in olfactory attraction to the box in the same way the ammonia did initially. Remove most solid waste from the box daily.

10. Locate the box in a confined area on a bare floor.

Select a suitable confinement area such as a bathroom, laundry room, wet bar area or sun room. If you prefer to place plastic, towels, newspaper or carpet underneath the box to protect a delicate floor, make sure it is the exact same size as the box. Don't give your cat a choice other than her box by placing carpet, rugs, newspaper or potty pads around the box.

11. Eliminate scent triggers from the environment.

In all cases, this step is essential to the success of the CATPAN 2000© program. The program will not work if this is not accomplished to at least 98%. It will be necessary to treat each and every accident your cat has had outside of the box. Urinary accidents can be accurately located with the use of an ultraviolet light. These lights can be purchased in a hand-held model at hardware stores for about $10, pet stores for $15 to $50, or on line.

Under no circumstances should ammonia be used to clean the target areas. As previously stated, ammonia is a component of urine. It will *attract* the cat to the wrong area for elimination.

You must use an odor remover to completely eliminate the odor in the carpets or furniture to the *cat's* sense of smell. If you can still smell it, so can your cat. Perfume sprays will only mask the odor and the litterbox problem will most likely return when the odor eventually returns.

There is a relatively new product on the market called Zero Odor Pet by Zero Odor, LLC, which is quite effective. It is non-toxic and biodegradable and available on line or at Bed Bath and Beyond. A 16-ounce spray bottle is about $15. Plain water followed by Zero Odor will pretty much eliminate odors.

Common household cleaners such as Resolve, Febreeze, Lysol, Pine-Sol or soap coat the molecules of waste so that odor remover may not work. In such case, use a 50/50 mixture of white vinegar and water to rinse off the molecules, use towels, newspaper or a wet vac to dry the area, then re-treat with odor remover.

You may have a cleaning method you believe works best for you. Here is ours.

11a. To clean urinary accidents from carpet

Use folded paper towels to press on the stain to draw the liquid *up and out* of the carpet. Pouring liquids on top of it will only serve to spread both the stain and the odor. If the spot is dry, mist plain water on it to moisten it so that it will wick up into the paper towels. Spray and repeat until what you are soaking up is clean, clear and not yellow. Dry the area as much as possible, then follow with the Zero Odor and let dry.

11b. To clean solid waste from carpet

Remove the waste and its residue, spray lightly underneath with Zero Odor and let dry.

In extreme cases the services of a professional carpet cleaning company may be necessary. Make a request that they not only treat the carpet, but also the padding underneath (or replace the padding), and the floor underneath that. Also ask them to apply cleaning product to the tack strip to which your carpet is secured, or replace it. This strip is usually raw wood and can retain enough odor to encourage the cat to continue to use the area for the wrong purpose. In severe cases, it may be necessary to fully replace the carpet, padding and tack strip.

It should be noted that a solidly box-trained cat (or well housetrained dog) will override a tiny bit of waste odor in the carpet and go where they should anyway. There is no need to drive yourself crazy over odor removal, simply do it as thoroughly as you can.

It should also be noted that if you have a cat and a dog, a cat will always go against something – a wall or a cabinet – whereas a dog will go in the center of a room. Don't blame the cat for something the dog has done.

12. Lay a protective cover over clean target areas.

Once you have done all the cleaning, there is nothing more frustrating than having the cat go right back and soil again on the cleaned areas. The point of the plastic is to protect the clean floor or carpet and prevent you from having to clean all over again. We like to take this step at this point in the program in case the cat escapes confinement (Step 14). If you are certain that won't happen, steps 12 and 13 can wait until the testing phase of the program, or Exit Program, is undertaken.

The majority of cats (and dogs) will naturally choose a soft, absorbent surface such as carpet or furniture for inappropriate elimination. A plastic covering will change the surface in the cat's perception and thus help to deter elimination in the area. This, in turn, will help break the cat's connection with the target area.

You can use plastic painters' drop cloths or plastic leaf bags on both the furniture and carpeted floors. If your cat has a large, carpeted target area, such as all around the walls of the dining room, we recommend covering the entire room, even the center of the floor. If you should happen to have one of those cats who is very determined to paw under the plastic and goof anyway, secure the edges of the plastic to the walls or baseboards with painter's tape.

If you are treating scent-marking, start the plastic about two feet above the floor on walls or furniture and run it down and out along the floor about three feet. Scent-markers want to get right up against that vertical surface for their spraying. See next step to discourage this.

13. Place food bowls or a strata deterrent on top of the plastic.

The objectives of this step are twofold: 1) to break the cat's connection with the target area(s), and 2) to discourage elimination in the area. There are three ways to accomplish this step.

    a) Place feeding bowls on top of the plastic.
    b) Place a strata deterrent on top of the plastic.
    c) Spray or place a scent deterrent on top of the plastic

a) Food bowl method

Cats will not eliminate where they eat. Placing their food bowls in their target areas can work easily and efficiently. The problem with this solution usually occurs in households where both dogs and cats reside. Dogs just love cat food with its high fat content, so placing cat food around for free doggie access may not be a workable solution. If it is a workable solution, do not use scent or step deterrents along with the food bowls. Use only the food bowls to break your cat's connection with the target area or areas.

b) Strata or step deterrent method

Strata is a layer or cover. A strata deterrent is a layer or cover placed on top of your carpet that a cat will avoid stepping on.

We think the best available strata deterrent is carpet runner placed upside down. You see carpet runner in model homes. It is made of clear, heavy plastic which is designed to protect the carpet of model homes from foot traffic. The underside of these runners is covered with tiny bumps to prevent the plastic runners from sliding around on the carpet. If you place the runner upside down, cats will absolutely refuse to walk on it. If they do, it will only be once.

Carpet runner can be purchased at home improvement stores. Costs will vary. It comes on rolls about 27 inches wide and costs approximately $2 or $3 per linear foot. It can be trimmed with scissors to fit your target area.

We suggest placing the carpet runner over the sheets of smooth plastic because the carpet runner is heavy plastic that does not always lie flat. If a cat were to urinate on it, the potential is high that the urine would run off the edges and right onto your cleaned carpet. Hence, the plastic underneath.

CAUTION: NEVER UNDER ANY CIRCUMSTANCES SHOULD SCAT MATS BE USED, EVER. Scat mats are plastic mats embedded with wires that can be plugged into an electrical outlet. The mats have three settings, low, medium and high. When a cat (or dog) steps on the mat it delivers a painful and terrifying electrical shock to the paws. Use of these mats inflicts serious trauma on the cat and will work against your program, perhaps irreversibly. Do not use scat mats as a deterrent.

c) Scent deterrent method

Placing or spraying a scent deterrent onto the runner now will aid in future steps of the program. We have found eucalyptus spray the best scent deterrent, available at whole food, health food or craft stores, or scent and candle shops. A small two-ounce bottle should cost around $6 to $10. Only a small amount is necessary, but you may find it necessary to repeat the use of eucalyptus daily. Another scent deterrent is any kind of citrus – lemon or orange peels.

Now your target areas are cleaned and your plastic protection, strata deterrent and scent deterrents are in place. On to the next step.

14. Extinguish the errant behavior and create a new habit with the use of confinement.

The ultimate objective of the entire CATPAN 2000© behavior program is to convince the cat to return to the litterbox. This step of the program forces the cat back into the box. This in turn changes her strata orientation back to litter for elimination, thus completing your ultimate objective. You can't skip this step and have any hope for success.

It must be made clear that the purpose of confinement is *not* to put the cat in jail as punishment. The purpose of the confinement is to change the strata orientation, or the surface the cat is accustomed to using for elimination, and return her to seeking out cat litter as her surface of choice for elimination. Confinement invites two weeks of unfailing use of the litterbox.

Your cat need not be confined endlessly for two weeks. She can be out of confinement any time you can supervise her. If she is sitting on your lap, she need not be confined. However if she gets off your lap and leaves the room, you'd best follow her to be certain her intentions are not devious. Confine her only when you cannot watch her. This might be overnight, while you are away at work during the day, or when you are in the shower or napping. If your cat has an accident in an inappropriate area during the confinement phase of the program, think of this as your mistake, not hers.

In all cases this confinement step is essential to the success of the CATPAN 2000© program. CATPAN 2000© will fail without this step. This is the one element of the program clients have an emotional problem with, more of a problem than the cats do. In the cases we have completed, long-term adverse behavioral side effects from the confinement have never been found to occur.

The material or surface a cat is standing on for elimination is more important than people think. In one case, on her first night of confinement, the poor little cat held her bladder all night long. In the morning when the owner let her out, she made a beeline for the surface she was accustomed to using: a potty pad inside the shower in another bathroom. The cat did this for two nights – not healthy for her.

On the third night, we had the owners cut one of her soiled potty pads in half and placed it on top of the litter inside her box. She used it. Over the ensuing week we gradually trimmed the potty pad until it was small enough to remove. The cat then continued to use the litterbox and not wait for her potty pad. We had changed the cat's strata orientation. The case was successful.

In another case, a feral kitten was adopted. He refused to use the litter in confinement. It was not what he was accustomed to and did not recognize it as a place to deposit his waste. We spread a few leaves, sticks and grass across the top of his litter. He immediately recognized the scent and texture of the leaves he had been using outdoors, and used the box. The kitten then continued to use the litterbox, even after the leaves and grass were gradually removed. His strata orientation had been changed. The case was successful.

Confinement Procedure

Choose a suitable confinement area. This may be a bathroom, wet bar, laundry room, large closet or small bedroom. If your choices are limited, a large cat cage may be used. The cage must be large enough to accommodate the litterbox, food, water, toys and a scratching post, and must also be large enough or have enough shelving to separate the box from food and water.

Confine the cat in a small area such as a bathroom or a laundry room with her box, food, water, toys, scratching post and a bed for two weeks. The floor under the box must be bare or, if carpeted, covered completely with plastic. Try not to leave a cat in confinement longer than about two weeks. Do not use scent deterrent inside the confinement area with the cat.

The smaller the confinement area, the greater potential your cat will use her box faithfully during the confinement period. However the larger the area, the more comfortable cat owners are about the confinement element of the program. If you have a large room your cat has never on any occasion used for inappropriate urination, defecation or spraying, you may use this area for your cat's confinement. This may be your bedroom, a sunroom or guest bedroom. Be sure to keep the food and water away from the box, and hope the cat does not find a new place to soil inappropriately. Check thoroughly for new spots after the cat has been alone for any period of time.

If you put a cat bed in the confinement area, it is best placed up on a counter. Both cats and dogs will choose any soft surface for elimination. If the bed is on the floor, your cat may use it instead of her litterbox. If there is no counter in the confinement area, a footstool or ottoman can hold the cat's bed up off the floor.

In one stubborn case, the cat was confined to the entry hall of the home. He was given only a carpeted foot stool for sitting or sleeping. His box was placed on the floor right next to the footstool. The rest of the floor we covered with air conditioning filters, the only thing this cat would not step on or eliminate on (we had not yet discovered the idea of upside down carpet runner). The case took longer than two weeks, but the cat eventually went back into his box for elimination. The case was successful.

If the confinement area is carpeted, it may or may not be necessary to cover entire floor with plastic and secure it around walls. We do not suggest carpet runner in the confinement area. Even though in a recent case this was necessary -- and successful -- we want to protect the floor only with plastic.

FROM BAD CAT TO GOOD CAT IN 21 DAYS

In a confined area most cats will not use the carpet and will only use the box for elimination, but there are exceptions. There is the occasional cat who will not take one step on plastic. If you have one of these cats, it definitely would not be practical to cover the entire carpeted floor in her confinement area. Whether or not you will need to cover the floor in the confinement area depends on your cat. You will find out the first night of confinement which one you have.

If in the past your cat has used the tub or the sink for elimination, leave a few inches of water standing in each. If she has used the shower, put her litterbox inside the shower. You want to make her litterbox her only choice for elimination.

If you are treating scent-marking, either provide a box with very high sides, or protect the walls around the box by taping up plastic and draping it down and into the box so the urine will run down the plastic and into the box. Pile cat litter over the bottom part of the plastic that drapes into the box to hold it in place. Over the two-week confinement period, we have found that spraying turns progressively back into squatting for urination.

Be very gentle about taking your cat into her confinement area. We do not want your cat to think she is being punished. Remember, this is not jail, it is simply placing the cat in an environment where she is most likely to begin to use her box again.

We are always confused by the high number of CATPAN 2000© users who do not seem to read the next sentence. ***Use treats to take your cat into her confinement area.*** Even if you don't think you need them, the treats are used not necessarily as a lure, but largely to create a positive association for going into confinement. You want confinement to mean pleasant things for your cat. So does your cat.

If you choose not to use treats to put your cat into confinement, be prepared: in about three days you may have a cat running and hiding from you when it is time for you to leave for work. She should not think you are angry with her, but you will get angry if you are late for work because you've been hunting down your cat. Just use a few flakes of tuna or chicken on top of her dry food, a bit of lunch meat, a teaspoon of wet cat food, some Kitty Kaviar®, or freeze-dried salmon or chicken. Use a treat she never gets any other time. If you choose to use treats, you may have a cat running to meet you in her confinement area every morning, and a cat who cries much less while in confinement.

Guard against being overly emotional about putting your cat into confinement. She will not mind it as much if you are not giving off signals of alarm. It's only for two weeks. If your cat cries to get out, ignoring this behavior should cause it to extinguish anywhere from an hour or two to a day or two after initial confinement. You can respond to her cries once at the beginning just to comfort her, but if you continue to respond to her cries, she will cry the entire two weeks. It is acceptable to go in and play, cuddle or groom, or let her out with full supervision. If you are going to let her out, it is best to wait until she is quiet for a minute so that you do not reinforce her complaining. Waiting until she is quiet reinforces the quiet behavior.

If your cat has *never* had an accident during the night she need not be confined at night. The reverse is also true. But if her accidents have occurred at all hours of the day or night, she must be confined during those hours. Your objective is to completely prevent elimination outside the box for a period of at least two weeks.

If your cat is an indoor/outdoor cat, we recommend *against* permitting her outdoors unsupervised during the confinement phase of the program. Letting her perform outside may not solve her indoor box problem.

In multi-cat households, obtain an additional litterbox for placement in the confinement area with the offending cat so that the cats who are not confined will continue to have a box of their own in its usual place. It will not be necessary to keep the other cats out of the offending cat's confinement area litterbox. Oftentimes the other cats in the house will be curious about the new setup and may go into the confinement area when it is open to use the box in there. This is perfectly acceptable.

In the case of two or more cats who are closely bonded, separation from one another can increase anxiety in the offending cat. In this case it is acceptable to confine the cats together, as confinement will not adversely affect the non-offending cat or cats.

If you find you have a cat who hurts herself trying to dig out of confinement, try making the confinement area larger, going into the area to play with her, or let her out to be with you but only on a leash and dog harness for close supervision. You can also use stacked baby gates instead of closing the door. We all know how much some cats hate a closed door.

15. Exercise your cat 15-20 minutes daily in the form of play.

If punishment has occurred, play will help your cat learn to trust you again. Evidence suggests that animals, like humans, release endorphins during exercise. This gives them a sense of well-being and reduces anxiety.

Play only with toys and *never* with your hands. Try to get your cat to jump or run using feathers on a fishing pole, a cotton rope or shoelace dragged along the floor, or a Fly Toy. Some cats respond avidly to the beam of a laser light or flashlight running around the floor. Some like to chase a child's soap bubbles through the air, still others like a ball of foil dropped on the kitchen floor or a ping pong ball in a dry bathtub. If your cat responds to catnip (some don't), get some fresh catnip and let her play with that for about fifteen minutes. If you have an older cat or an overweight cat who simply refuses to move, you may just have to skip this step.

16. Repair broken bonds by giving your cat thirty minutes of quality time daily.

The objective of this step is to counteract the isolation of confinement and repair any bonds that have been broken due to scolding, spanking or squirting. Quality time should be split between brushing her, just sitting with her and petting her, and teaching her tricks. If you have a cat who will not tolerate petting or brushing, start by stroking her while she's eating. If you have a very smart cat, or a dog trapped in a cat's body, teach her something daily, such as sit up, shake hands, roll over, speak, jump through a hoop, climb a ladder. Use treats and work with her the same way you would a dog, or use clicker training. It may surprise some people that cats can actually learn obedience. On the contrary. The cat learning process is exactly the same as dogs.

17. Address any residual anxiety in the environment.

The objective of this program is to remove all possible sources of the cat's anxiety. If there are other pets in the household your offending cat is not getting along with, you must address this. Hold counter-conditioning sessions between the two pets, associating positive things such as treats, brushing or catnip, if your cats are susceptible to catnip, with the presence or approach of the other. To be safe, have the aggressor on a leash and dog harness, or use baby gates between them.

If your cat's anxiety is caused by outdoor strays your cat can see through the window, use a scent, sound or water deterrent to eliminate this as a source of your cat's anxiety. Deter outdoor cats from your yard by spraying chili pepper, pepper spray or eucalyptus around where they like to go. Impulse sprinklers can be extremely effective at keeping stray cats out of your yard, but your setup has to be just right. Sound devices silent to humans but unpleasant to cats can also be obtained at a hardware store or pest control service. If removing the outdoor cats from your territory is not possible, then try to remove them at least from your own cat's view by closing the blinds or drapes and providing an alternate window for your cat to sit by.

18. (*Optional*) Allow your cat outdoors at least 15-20 minutes daily, supervised of course.

Earlier we mentioned that we do not suggest letting your cat outside during the program. To clarify, we do not want the cat roaming free on her own outdoors. The outings suggested here are supervised only. Cats should never be allowed to roam outdoors without your supervision.

The objective of this step is to counteract boredom. Many cats do not respond well to 'domestication,' i.e., bringing her inside, altering her, removing her claws (NEVER do this!), and closing the door permanently behind her. Getting a cat outside activates at least four new avenues of stimulation and will do wonders for many cats.

If you are nervous that your cat might bolt away from you and into the woods, you can put her on a long leash attached to a V-neck dog harness, *not a cat harness*. Some cats will initially object to the use of a harness, but the joy of outdoor stimulation usually overrides in a matter of moments.

If your cat is terrified of the outdoors, forcing the issue would only increase anxiety and defeat your purpose of *decreasing* anxiety. If this describes your cat, you should skip this step.

Over the next two weeks, watch for the following signs in your cat.

- Actively seeking out box and using it openly
- More thorough covering in the box
- An increase in self-grooming
- More affectionate to owners and/or visitors
- Happier
- More playful
- More tolerant to handling
- More resilient, less 'jumpy'

Whether or not your cat has had an accident or two during the confinement phase of the program, you can continue on to Phase II. However if her accidents outside the box occurred in the second week or even the final few days of confinement, she is not yet ready for her final exam and confinement should be continued a few days longer.

Please note

This program has been scientifically tested on more than 200 cats. Time periods are critical. We strongly advise *against* giving your cat free access to the environment and her target areas too early just to "see what she'll do." This will delay your program and may damage it to the point of no return. We have had a number of programs fail because owners thought they knew best and chose to test the cat before the prescribed time. You only have one shot at this program for full effect. We have found that starting the same program over again is never quite as effective the second time around.

CHAPTER TWO

The Exit Program
A Crucial Step

In all cases of inappropriate elimination in cats, the cat must be 'tested' in order to confirm her rehabilitation. Cat owners cannot be expected to spend the rest of their lives with plastic or litterboxes all over the house, and a cat cannot spend the rest of her life in confinement. If you never test her, you will never know if you have achieved success

This second phase of CATPAN 2000© may be the singular reason CATPAN 2000© succeeds where other programs fail.

The objective of the Exit Program is to see whether your cat will continue to choose inappropriate areas for elimination or instead go back to her box. This part of the program simply involves gradually permitting your cat access to her old target areas. It is quite possible that the reason this program works where others fail is its careful attention to detail during the release and testing phase of the program.

Many cat owners have previously tried confinement for their offending cats, usually on the advice of their veterinarian, but the advice stops there. They find that the cat uses her box flawlessly in the confinement area, however after the confinement period when the cat is given back her freedom, she goes right back to her old habits. This is because the new behavior of using the litterbox was never stabilized. The previous errant behavior was triggered by inattentiveness to the necessity of a gradual release. In such case the entire program must be started again. As previously stated, experience has shown that a second program undertaken in immediate succession to a first, failed program is rarely successful. It is therefore critical that you ease out of the Phase I program with Phase II.

After ten days to two weeks of confinement you should begin to see signs your cat is ready to be tested. She may be covering more thoroughly in the box, grooming more, friendlier, more affectionate, more tolerant to handling, more playful, and actively and unabashedly seeking out the litterbox. You should see at least one of these signs before testing. Even if you don't, test her anyway.

If you have more than one offending cat, test one cat at a time. This is the only way to confirm with certainty who is rehabbed and who is not. Instead of testing each cat fourteen days, you can shorten the Exit Program by testing each cat about four or five days, then re-confining her and testing the next one.

Curiously, we have seen no adverse effects from re-confining a rehabilitated cat while testing a second or third cat.

If you have a cat who only offends at night and can be free in the day in your absence without mishap, you will only be testing her at night. The opposite is also true. If you have a cat who is not choosy about the time of day to miss the litterbox, you can test her for nighttime first while you continue to confine her in the day in your absence. After five nights without an accident, then test her five days for cleanliness during the day.

Some cat owners are more comfortable testing their cats in gradually increasing areas of the house instead of just letting the cat out into the entire house and then having to search for accidents. Other cat owners just go for it. Which way you do it is up to you, and may depend on the size of your house. To test for smaller areas at a time, just use closed doors or stacked baby gates to prevent her access to further areas of the house. Then you can gradually open doors or remove baby gates to permit more freedom until she is clean in the whole house.

CHAPTER THREE

PHASE II
The Exit Program Procedure

The overlying cause of a failed cat litterbox retraining program in a healthy cat is the failure to test gradually for successful rehabilitation.

Phase II Objectives

- Gradually permit the cat access to target areas.
- Re-confine for premature accidents.
- Assure that the cat is fully retrained to use box at all times.

Before beginning Phase II, be certain of the following.

1. Cat is in good health.

2. Waste odors have been removed from the environment.

3. Strata deterrent (plastic, upside down carpet runners or other flat objects your cat won't want to step on) are placed over target areas.

4. Scent deterrent has been sprayed or placed on strata deterrent in target areas.

    (Optional) The cat litter may be completely changed out at this point, but continue to use natural clay litter. Repeat ammonia treatment once.

PHASE II PROCEDURE

1. Take your cat to her confinement area with her treat as usual, but leave the door ajar. Continue to take her into confinement for the first three to five mornings or nights of testing.

You will want the transition from confinement to freedom to be as subtle as possible. You want your cat to 'discover' she is free to roam her target areas. Be certain to prop the door to prevent it from closing accidentally. Blocking a cat's re-entry to the litterbox area during the testing program is a sure way to start the problem all over again.

Your cat may bounce out of her room right behind you. If she does, ignore her and go on to work or bed as though you had confined her.

After 3-5 (clean) days of 'pretending' to confine her, this practice may be discontinued and you can simply leave her free to roam. Again, you may choose to close off some rooms so that you don't have such a large area to check for mistakes at the end of the day. In this way your cat can gradually 'earn' her freedom one room at a time.

2. Upon your return, darken the target room and check for accidents with an ultra-violet light source.

Checking with the light is the only way to know for certain whether your cat has passed her first test. Odor can take 2-3 months to build up enough for you to detect by simply sniffing the air. Just shine the light around all areas near walls to be sure your cat has not found a new target area. Liquid stains will show up greenish-yellow in the light. As each day passes, you must be absolutely certain that your cat has neither used an old target area nor found a new one.

3. If you find elimination has occurred outside the box, treat the spot for odor and re-confine your cat for three more days or nights, then test again.

We have had cases in which relapses occurred as many as three times. A couple of relapses are to be expected. Don't get discouraged. Eventually cats seem to associate their accidents with their re-confinement and the problem clears up. (A three-day period of re-confinement will also be used for any future backsliding. This will be explained later.)

4. Each 'clean' day earns another day free of confinement.

Continue to check for accidents the entire fourteen days. If and whether your cat relapses on the 6th day or the 9th day or the 13th day, re-confine her three days and start the count over.

5. After fourteen days of unfailing use of the litterbox for elimination while free of confinement, begin to gradually remove the plastic and carpet runner from the target areas.

Since all kitty accidents occur at or on the walls, begin in the center of the room and fold the plastic back toward the walls one to two feet a day, leaving the strongest target areas covered the longest. The number of days it takes to completely remove the plastic depends on the size of the room and the number of target areas. Gradually removing the plastic usually takes three to ten days.

If you have used the food bowls as a deterrent, remove the plastic from underneath first, then remove one bowl each day until gone.

6. After the process of gradually removing the plastic and carpet runner has been completed, leave the scent deterrent (or food bowls) in the target areas for an additional week.

Leaving the scent deterrent in the uncovered target areas will complete the process of breaking your cat's connection to the target areas. If you are treating scent-marking, Feliway may be used in the target areas at this point. This is optional. Feliway may or may not make a difference in your cat's behavior. We have had mixed results with this product.

7. Remove the plastic or other strata deterrents from the confinement area.

If it was necessary to cover a carpet inside the cat's confinement area, this may be removed all at once. Do not use a scent deterrent in the confinement area at any time.

8. Gradually re-locate the litterbox to the permanent location.

If it has been necessary to change the location of the box into the confinement area for the period of the program, wait until this point to begin moving it slowly, a few feet per day, back to the desired location. If you move the box gradually, your cat will stay with her box and 'follow' it back to the location you desire. If she has an accident right behind it, you have tried to move the box too fast.

Some cats can simply be shown the new location of the box and stay on it. Others need to have the box moved gradually.

9. Gradually phase out quality time, daily brushing and play.

It is best not to 'jump' off the program. Drop a session per week of quality time, leveling off at a minimum of three sessions per week for healthy maintenance. However, discontinuing the quality time, grooming, teaching, play and outdoor jaunts is optional. We have found that, time permitting, most CATPAN 2000© users have been pleasantly surprised by their cats' response to these activities and most prefer to continue some or all of them.

10. If desired, re-introduce box cover, liners and preferred litter type at this point.

If any one of these items causes the litterbox problem to recur, discontinue its use permanently.

11. If the cat relapses in the future, take the following steps.

In the case of future relapses, we have found it unnecessary to repeat the entire program from the beginning.

Procedure for future relapses

Check the cat for medical problems to rule out all possible medical causes. Treat the spot or spots for odor with plain water and Zero Odor only. Cover target area with plastic and scent deterrent. Prevent further accidents for ***three days*** by confining the cat with litterbox, food, water, a bed, post and toys. Then repeat the Exit Program for about three or four days to a week.

As a future preventative measure with cats who are prone to anxiety, use three days of confinement when dramatic changes take place in your environment. To a cat, 'dramatic changes' can be major events such as a marriage, adding a baby or new pet to the family, or moving/relocating.

Note to veterinarians and cat owners:

In every case of the failure of this program, we have found a chronic medical condition to exist. These conditions have included diabetes, thyroid

problems, epilepsy, hip dysplasia, blockages, stones, etc. In the case of a cat experiencing four or more relapses during the Exit Program, meaning the cat is not testing out successfully, we unequivocally recommend a more in-depth medical examination to determine the cause of the medical anxiety that is preventing successful litterbox re-entry. We have found that once these conditions were treated and the symptoms relieved, in almost all cases rehabilitation was successful.

Many thanks to each of the hundreds of cat owners who unknowingly contributed to making this program a success.

FROM BAD CAT TO GOOD CAT IN 21 DAYS

We wish you the best of luck with CATPAN 2000©. With it we have achieved success in 99% of completed cases of defecation, 98% of urination, and 96% of scent-marking. CATPAN 2000© carries a 98% guarantee.

We do understand that cats are individually unique. If you have a particular problem or question that we have not foreseen, please feel welcome to e-mail Diane Arrington. Please be brief. Short questions will be addressed as a courtesy. If you need lengthy or repeated on-line counseling, you can use your Visa or MasterCard.

Diane Arrington
Founder/Director

PetPerfect Academy of Obedience
& Behavioral Science

972/484-8882

www.petperfect.com

dianearrington@petperfect.com

SUPPLY LIST

- ☐ Large litterbox
- ☐ Natural ground clay, unscented, non-clumping litter
- ☐ Plain ammonia
- ☐ Ultra violet light
- ☐ Scent remover
- ☐ Plastic sheeting
- ☐ Painter's tape
- ☐ Strata deterrent
- ☐ Scent deterrent
- ☐ Toys

QUICK-REFERENCE GUIDE

CATPAN 2000©
Copyright 1986, 2015 Diane Arrington

PHASE I - Retraining/Confinement

1. Rule out minor medical causes.
2. Stop all scolding or punishment of any kind.
3. Separate food and water from box.
4. Provide a large, uncovered, unlined litterbox.
5. Use natural ground clay litter, non-clumping and non-deodorized, 4-5 inches deep.
6. 'Bait' the litter with a few drops of plain ammonia.
7. Scoop and stir box daily; don't change litter for two weeks.
8. Eliminate all waste odors from environment.
9. Cover target areas with plastic.
10. Place strata deterrent over plastic.
11. Place or spray scent deterrent on target areas.
12. Confine cat in small area with box, food, water, toys and a bed for 14 days.

13. Exercise cat 15-20 minutes daily.

14. Give cat 30 minutes of quality time daily.

15. Address any residual anxiety in the environment.

PHASE II - Exit/Testing Program

1. Test cat by permitting access to target areas.

2. If soiling occurs outside box, re-confine three more days and test again.

3. Each clean day earns another day of freedom.

4. After 14 days clean, begin gradual removal of plastic and strata or scent deterrent.

5. After plastic is gone, leave scent deterrent one week.

6. Remove plastic from confinement area (as needed).

7. Reposition box gradually to original location (as needed).

8. Gradually phase out quality time and play (optional).

9. Reintroduce box cover, liner and preferred litter type.

ABOUT THE AUTHOR

Diane Arrington began her training and behavior practice for dogs and cats in 1980. She is Founder and Director of PetPerfect® Academy of Obedience and Behavioral Science in Dallas, Texas. She currently resides in Dallas with her two dogs and two cats. She can be reached through her website at petperfect.com.

www.ingramcontent.com/pod-product-compliance
Lightning Source LLC
Chambersburg PA
CBHW060507080526
44584CB00015B/1583